Hogs Back Books
– a nose for a good book …

For Eliza, Sam & Katie, and Sam & Emily – AB
For my Mom – NP

Published by
Hogs Back Books
34 Long Street, Devizes
Wiltshire
SN10 1NT
www.hogsbackbooks.com
Text copyright © 2017 Anna Best
Illustrations copyright © 2017 Natallia Pavaliayeva
The moral right of Anna Best to be identified as the author
and Natallia Pavaliayeva to be identified as the illustrator of this work has been asserted.
First published in Great Britain in 2017 by Hogs Back Books Ltd.
All rights reserved. No reproduction, copy or transmission
of this publication may be made without prior written permission.
No part of this publication may be reproduced, stored in a retrieval system,
or transmitted in any form or by any means, electronic, mechanical, photocopying,
recording or otherwise without the prior permission of the publisher.

Printed in Malta
ISBN: 978-1-907432-29-3
British Library Cataloguing-in-Publication Data.
A catalogue record for this book is available from the British Library.
1 3 5 4 2

Aunt Grizelda's Treasury of Grim and Grisly Rhymes

Anna Best • Natallia Pavaliayeva

Eliza and the spider

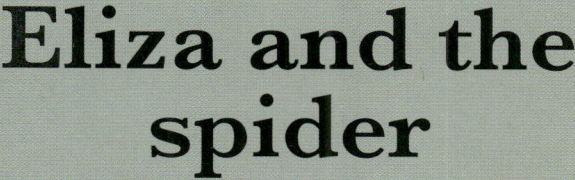

Eliza spied a spider,
It scuttled down the door
And settled down beside her,
Which made Eliza roar.

The spider felt offended.
He asked, "Why do you cry?
I'm just a little spider;
To me you're giant-sized!"

Eliza stopped her yelling –
The spider's words were true:
He wasn't really scary,
So she squished him with her shoe.

The lesson of this story
Is absolutely clear:
Don't advertise your weaknesses
When enemies are near.

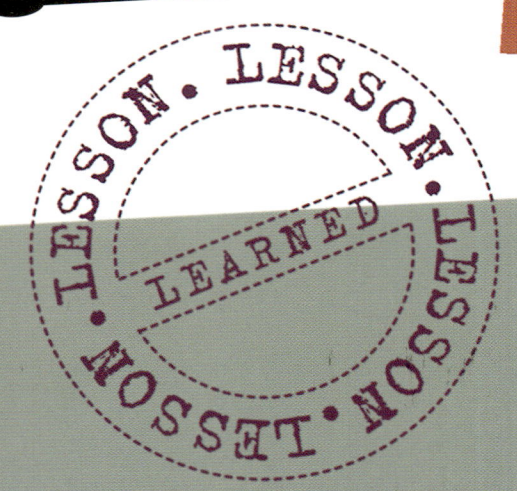

(Not so) smart phone

Dicey icy

"The ice looks nice," thought Lulu
As she walked beside the lake,
And so she stepped out onto it –
A terrible mistake;
The ice was far from sturdy,
In places wafer thin –
Before she'd gone three paces,
It cracked and she fell in.

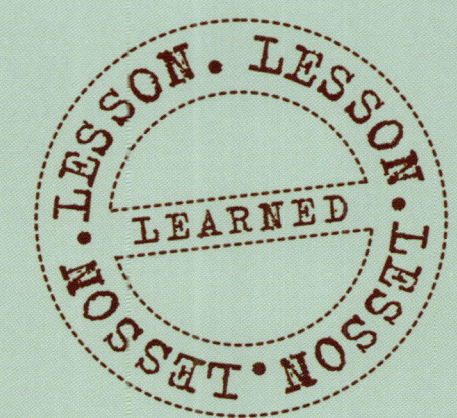

Down to the depths she drifted,
Where only fishes go,
And froze stiff as a statue,
Pale blue from head to toe.
Despite attempts to thaw her,
The ice, with iron will,
Held Lulu in its freezing grasp –
Alas! She's frozen still!

So when the snow has fallen
And turned the landscape white;
When girls and boys are sledging
And shrieking with delight;
Ice on a lake may tempt you,
May promise skating thrills,
But please remember icicles
Can soon be icy kills.

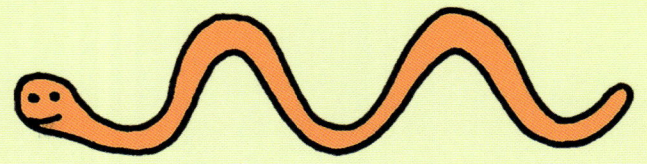

Diet of worms

Miranda, in her infancy,
Would often dine on worms for tea,
And sometimes in her childish greed
Would gobble up a centipede.
Or if, by chance, she saw a spider,
Within a jiff, it was inside her.
The delicacy she liked the most
Was black-slug pâté spread on toast.
On insects large and small she'd munch,
So most days she was out to lunch.

Her mother tried to remonstrate
About the things her daughter ate,
But Grandma said, "It's just her age;
She's only going through a stage,
And by the time she reaches four,
She won't eat insects anymore."

Well, time proved Grandma was correct –
She now treats insects with respect.
But sad to say, her current taste
Is mainly for the human race,
And now Miranda's rising ten,
She eats small boys and sometimes men.

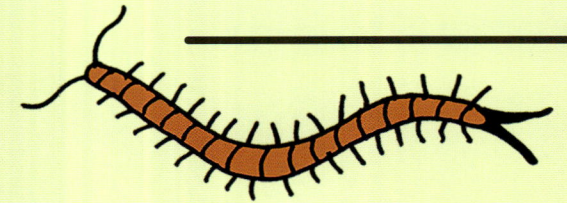

The reason why

There was a boy in days of old,
Who always did as he was told;
With any order he'd comply
And never asked the reason why.
One day a passing archer said,
"Pray, put this apple on your head,"
And being an obliging kid,
Why, that's exactly what he did.

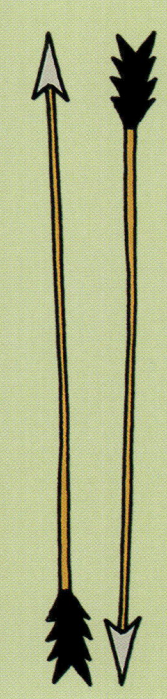

The archer – Robin Hood no less –
Was hoping that he would impress
And aimed to make the apple fall
Without touching the boy at all.

Now normally his shot went well
(He'd learned the trick from William Tell),
But when he let the arrow go,
It struck the boy a mortal blow.

The lesson you should learn hereby
Is always ask the reason why,
And do not be too meek and good,
Especially for Robin Hood.

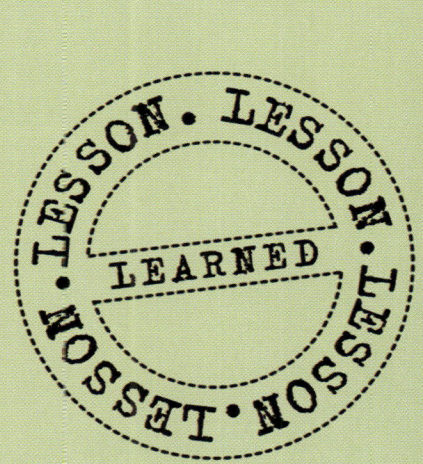

Computer game catastrophe

There was a lad named Silas,
His tale is sad to tell;
All day he played computer games –
It didn't turn out well.

His mind was set on levels,
On quests and foes and scores;
And even on the brightest day,
He never played outdoors.

Slowly he lost the roses
That in his cheeks once bloomed,
And looked more like a zombie
Just risen from its tomb.

It happened that one midnight
(It was at Halloween),
A claw reached out and grabbed him,
And pulled him through the screen.

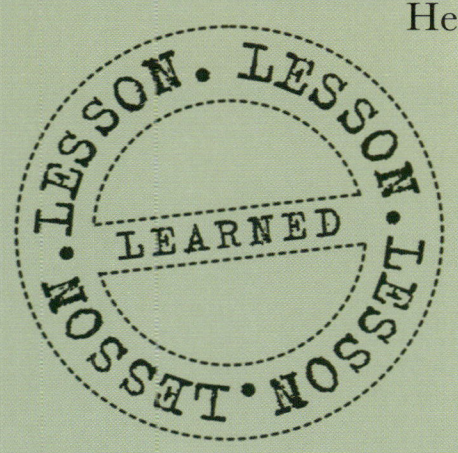

He screamed and shrieked, "Release me!
You know not what you do!
My home is in the 3D world;
I don't belong in two."

Alas! He was imprisoned
Within an Xbox game –
A creature made of pixels,
A boy only in name.

Pursued by ghosts and creepers,
Blown up by cosmic rays,
Poor Silas met destruction
A million different ways.

And to this day poor Silas
Inside the screen remains,
A warning to all addicts
Hooked on computer games.

So if you must play *Minecraft*,
The Walking Dead or *Doom*,
Please don't forget the real world
That lives outside your room.

Playing with fire

A foolish boy called Zebediah
Thought it fun to play with fire.
In a den, when it was dark,
Flicked a lighter, caused a spark:
Leaves and twigs at once ignited,
Zeb at first was much delighted;
But the fire he had made
Blazed right up and quickly strayed
Throughout the den, along the floor,
Cutting off the only door.
Zebediah's end was fated –
In the den incinerated.

Matches, lighters, candles too:
All three could be the death of you;
So please remember naked flames
Are not the stuff of children's games.

Puddled

Approach a puddle with great care,
For though it's sitting idly there
As if it could bring no one harm,
Do not be hoodwinked by its charm.

A puddle, as the whole world knows,
Is plotting how to soak your clothes
And fill your wellies with a flood
Of slippy, slimy, sloopy mud.

Young Dudley found a puddle, which
Was situated by a ditch.
He did not pause – he leapt straight in:
The water came up to his chin.

"Help! Help!" he cried, "I can't get out!"
The puddle smiled and oozed about.
The puddle grinned and thanked its luck
In getting Dudley firmly stuck.

And what was worse, the water stank
Of things malodorous and rank,
And people held their noses while
They tried to free the swampy child.

They pulled and tugged with all their might,
But Dudley's puddle held on tight,
And sad to say, they could not save
Poor Dudley from a boggy grave.

So when a puddle seems to say
"Come on, jump in!" you must delay,
And with a stick research how deep,
And always look before you leap.

Trainspotting

Beneath this stone lie the earthly remains
Of young Toddy Tumble, a spotter of trains.
He spotted each number with vigour and vim,
But the one that he missed was the one that got him.

So if you're a spotter of diesel or freight,
Remember young Toddy, his grisly fate,
And even when after a number you lack,
Be kind to your body and stay off the track.

Grizelda Schwarz was born on 31st October 1832 in Transylvania. After graduating with a degree in lycanthropy from Kreep University, she worked as a journalist for *Zombie Times* and then for the women's magazine *Haunted Homes*.

Grizelda is now a freelance writer and lives in a belfry on the Yorkshire Moors with her pet wolfhounds Fang and Baskerville, pipistrelle bat Squeaky, and serpents Bella and Donna.